MW00936187

Shared Wisdom

from an

Intuitive Spirit

D.J. Campbell

Welcome Kind Reader –
Before You Begin ...

Each message written in this book comes for many people. For many ask the same questions. They have the same concerns; the same doubts; the same worries. All are looking for answers, for guidance, for a message, for some inner wisdom from a higher place. The messages that are meant for you to hear, for you to receive are written amongst the pages of this book. Trust that your higher self will guide you to the message that you need to hear the most at this moment. In your moment. Close your eyes. Let your fingers run through the pages and stop where you feel you should. Read with your eyes, listen with your heart and hear with your soul. Keep the pieces you need to keep, hold on to those that resonate with you now. Allow those that do not be left for another day, another moment. Do not overthink, allow your inner wisdom to be your guide. Trust in this. Know that you will find your answers. You will find your truth.

...YOU

Now is the time for awareness. Be aware of your surroundings, the movement, the energies. Be aware of yourself – your breathing, your heartbeat, your body, but bring your awareness out further. Be aware of your thoughts, your feelings, your sense of self. Hear the voices, the conversations, the words, the phrases that run through your mind. Feel how they change, not only in their patterns, but in the way each thought changes you. Does your heart quicken? Does it make you smile? Does it make you angry? Lonely? Be aware of how it affects your soul. Realize that you are the one who has the control to choose, to decide which to keep and which to let go. With each thought, acknowledge it, be aware of it. Tell yourself "I love you" and decide to embrace or release each thought. Keep those that enhance you. Release those that demean you. Be aware of who you are. Be aware of what you are. Be aware of the connections around you and within you. Know that you have the power to determine how they affect you.

A new day has come. Many things are in the works for you. Many new adventures. Enjoy them as they come along. Savor each one slowly, fully as they are gifts for you. Keep your eyes open that you will see each and every blessing sent your way. Enjoy today and tomorrow and all the tomorrows that are brought to you. Live in the moment. Live fully in each and every moment. Take in as much as you can. Experience all that you can.

Know the rightness that is you. You are perfect just the way you are. Others are finally beginning to notice. You will see changes in their behavior. Several will be attracted to you. You will know which are sincere and which are not. You will have no doubts with your feelings.

Believe in yourself. That is your greatest beauty. That is your best feature. You have many beautiful traits, but your belief in you is the greatest, most attractive one. The positive energies you show create more positive energies. It allows others to show theirs, enjoy theirs. It invites them to be positive and confident as well. You are a role model for many. You set the standard for many. You set the goal for many to follow. Believe in yourself. You are beautiful, the light shines through you.

It is good you have released things from your past. Cleansing and clearing are always good things. Especially if they hold or harbor ill feelings. Your future will be filled with wonderful things. You are going to have a wonderful year. Believe this. Good things are coming. They've already started. You have put many things into motion when you decided to try new things.

It is normal, it is human to doubt, to question, to wonder "what if" – and it is especially normal for you to do that more than anyone else. It is part of your nature- it is part of your upbringing to question, to verify, to understand in a way only you can. This is good, it is a part of you, of who you are, but do not let it hinder you. Do not let it cause a block, create walls or make you doubt yourself. Ask for clarity – yes. Cause doubt and distress – no. That only makes your energy scattered. Stay aligned, stay true to your heart and your heart's desire. For it is a pure desire. One based out of love and caring. One of value and of honor.

Focus on you. Focus on the moment and live each moment fully, completely with the energy only you can provide. Just believe in yourself and let it run. Let it go. Let it happen.

You will find happiness, but only if you allow yourself to be happy. Find your happiness within yourself, for yourself, because of yourself. Find joy in yourself. Stop trying to find it in others. Find the happiness you seek in yourself. Experience the joy in life as <u>you</u>. "Easier said than done" you say. But it is only a matter of doing it. Stop thinking. Stop waiting for more to happen. Let it happen as it will. For it will. With or without you – and faster if it's without you. We see you struggle to do everything "right". You need not struggle. There is no right except what is right for you. Stay true to yourself. The rest will fall into place as it should and as it will. You think too much with your head. Let your heart, your intuitive, your gut lead you for a while.   Let your head rest. Stop trying to rely on logic. Let it be. Let it happen. Know that it is happening. You do not need to figure out the how's or why's or where's or even when's. Be present in you. The rest will follow.

Feel free to live your life. Enjoy your life. Enjoy yourself. Enjoy You. Dance until your heart's content. Laugh until you can laugh no more and when that time arrives, smile knowing that you are living your life as it is meant to be.

The morning light is shining in your window and as the sun illuminates your world, so will your light illuminate your universe. You <u>do</u> matter, everything you do, every action you take, every thought you think matters. You influence the universe and the world around you so much more than you realize. You have a power beyond measure. You affect everyone around you, in big ways, in subtle ways, but you affect them none the less. People are attracted to you because of your positive energy, your welcomed demeanor, your confidence. You can change the world around you with just a soft smile. That is why you are so amazing. That is why they are drawn to you. You are like a beacon, drawing people away from the fog of sadness, un-sur-ed-ness, everyday-ness to a warm, happy, positive place. You shine. You radiate. You GLOW. Those not able to get past the fear of doing something new and out of the ordinary watch you from afar. Yearning to be like you, with you, but still caught in that fear unable to break free. They are jealous of you and may even despise you. Do not fret over them. They have their own lessons to learn. Just seeing you – seeing that they could be like you is part of that lesson. You do not realize just how much you matter. You do matter. You do count. You will soon come to realize just exactly how much you do. You will understand your value. You will come to know your strength and power. You will see just how highly people appraise you. Lives will be change because of you.

We have told you many things, many wonderful things. Now is the time for you to see them come to fruition. It is time for your affirmation, your confirmation of all that you have heard and felt. It may take some time perhaps longer than you thought. But how completely full that time will be.

Blessed be this day. It marks the time that will bring you many wonderful things. Gifts from the heart, gifts for your soul, for your higher path. Many things will move quickly – almost a blur they will move so fast. Good things, all good things. You are a beautiful spirit. You bring love and positive energy wherever you go. It is wonderful, it is blessed and is a blessing. You will soon do even more. Bring even more into your life. When you are right with yourself, right with your spirit, aligned and on your path, many, many blessings begin to show. And you will bring blessings to others. It is your way, it is your gift.

Reveal. Rediscover what is inside of you and use the opportunities that are there. You only have to see and believe. Believe and see to make them appear. God has so much in store for you – if you only let it happen.

Love your life. Enjoy your life. Celebrate it for all to see. Shine that light. Do not cover it, protect it or hide it from the world. The strength of your light does not depend on the strength of others nor do you need others for your light to shine. Your light is strong. Your light is your own. It needs no other to shine brightly. Shine your light, yes – but do not depend on another for its fuel.

A new life is starting for you. One with a new focus. A focus on you and no one else. The time to focus on others is over. You are no longer needed to guard over them. That is someone else's job now. You have done your job well. You have grown much during this time. Now is the time to focus on you and your life. Your life is to change. This holding pattern you have placed yourself in is done. It is no longer needed. Allow yourself to be set free. Spread your wings and fly. Soar as you were meant to soar. You are now un-tethered. No one is holding your back any longer.

You have done well. Times were hard, your test was difficult. But you kept your honor and fared well. You are strong. Your spirit is strong. Weaker ones would have turned, yet you did not. You are a child of light. Your spirit is of the light and shall always be.

Your dreams await. You will feel free to do anything your heart can imagine. Your path has been spread before you. It feels right doesn't it? It feels good, does it not? You can feel the positive vibrations running through you now. Each breath is alive with the energy. It feels good, it feels natural. It feels true, it rings true. Do not doubt. Do not question. It is true. It is great. It is good.

A choice is to be made, and you will make it easily and completely. Just follow your heart. Let it guide you. Your day is coming. Your time is on its way. You will find the peace within. Believe in yourself. Believe in what you can do. What you are doing. Demand the best, for you deserve the best. Let the universe bring the best to you. For it is your right, your destiny. Live well, love well. Do this and what you seek will be found. It will come to you.

You are blessed. You are gifted in many ways and in many more that you have yet to discover. Trust yourself. Trust your talent; your gift; your blessing. Like the petals of a rose, more and more of you will be revealed as you blossom, as you grow. Your true beauty, your true talent is yet to be revealed. Many layers. Many pieces yet to show themselves. All combined into one beautiful prize. Allow yourself the fulfillment of you. Allow yourself the right to be you. It's ok to be special, because you are. Allow yourself all the blessings given to you to use. Realize your worth. Realize your value. Realize just how special you are and accept that you ARE special. Allow yourself to know, truly know exactly who you are and what you can accomplish. Accept all that is you. Embrace everything you have to offer. You have much to do. Believe you can get it done. For you can and you will.

Look to your future for it is a bright one. Your energies are clear and at their highest potential. Believe in yourself and believe in your dreams for it is you who will bring power to them as you believe in the possibilities. Yes, aim high for that is the goal you must set. And reach them you will. What you envision, what you have seen in your mind's eye is just the beginning of things yet to come. You need not search for answers outside of yourself for those lie within. Look inside, you will find what you need. Your higher self knows this already. It is time for you to allow yourself to know as well.

Why hold on to self-doubt? Why question the blessings that are yours - the blessing that is you? Believe. Believe with all that is within you. Believe IN all that IS you. Do not discount your abilities. You have talents and strengths so vast, so varied. Do not start to doubt yourself. Keep believing in yourself. You are coming into your own. All new, wonderful things are in store for you and coming to you. Accept it. Acknowledge it. Enjoy it. Give thanks for it. Most of all HONOR it. Honor you. FOCUS. Breathe and focus. Hear your inner self, your true self. You have much knowledge inside you. Knowledge of several lifetimes. Knowledge of the universe. All there for you to use, to refer to – to hear if you'd only listen.

Allow yourself to hear, to feel, to see all that is within you for it is a beautiful thing. You are a beautiful creation. Know that you are cared for. All needs are taken care of. Whatever is needed is brought to you when it is needed. You know this truth. The beauty of this truth lies deep inside you along with the courage and the faith that comes from your innermost knowledge. Hold true to yourself. Hold true to your heart. Believe. Know.

Do not fret. This is to be. it will not be difficult or painful. But it is one of the decisions you must make along your path – a fork in the road – as you have come across before. Pivotal moments that define who you are and who you want to be. You will move through this gracefully, almost effortlessly. Follow your heart – not your head – do not think things through to oblivion. You could get lost in the details and never find your way. Be aware the moment is near, that pivotal moment is at hand. Now, above anything else, be true to yourself. Hold on to the "who" you are, and all that you stand for. Don't lose yourself during this confusion, this "chaos". When you make your choice- remember what you know. Your heart will guide you, your soul, your higher self will guide you if you just allow it to happen. You will find what you seek. You will find your happiness – your happiness will find you. Do not try to read anything into what you see or hear. When it happens, it will be so obvious, you will know the minute it arrives. You have been told of its coming and with that you know that you have been prepared. You will not be shocked, not be thrown, not be caught off guard. We tell you these things so you will be prepared and ready. Go in Grace with this knowledge. Act with Grace. Choose wisely, choose well as we know you will.

Believe in your light, your power, your goodness. All things happen for a reason. All things in their own time. Your time is coming. Your time to shine is coming. Take the time to allow your inner peace to come to you. Let that be your mindset. Do not allow the season's darkness to affect you as you are. Season's change, you know this. The weather is as the weather is. You are you. You are who allow yourself to be. Pull the inner peace forward.

Today is a day to establish value. Value in yourself. What is your worth? What are your riches? Yes, you have many. What are your strengths? What are your talents? What are your gifts? What blessings have you received? List them. Acknowledge them. Feel them. Be proud of them. All are wonderful and powerful in their own right. Now look back at yourself and your life. Decide for yourself. Is there truly lack? Or have you devalued yourself by deception?

Everyone is on a path. You each have a path to walk. All paths are sacred; all paths have a purpose. A journey of discovery and growth. A journey that takes you to places you have never been and also returns you to places you have seen before. There are moments with traveling companions and there are others that you must travel alone. Trails often intersect for a time, then wind away only to intersect once again when the time is right. Travelers may have paths that cross only once for a brief moment in their lifetimes, while others will find their roads winding to and fro, intersecting and weaving many shared moments throughout their journey. Some parallel each other, glancing at each other in the distance, but never really meeting at all, others intersect and merge as one until the end. You have walked many paths, journeyed along many trails. But the most important part of all your travels is this time, this place, where you are now. Savor each step. Take it all in with open eyes. Do not run headlong and blindly, blundering along the way. Take the time that is needed to live each moment fully. There will be many very important moments. Don't miss a single one.

Smile. Laugh. Live. That is all you need to know and all you need to do at this time. Enjoy life. Enjoy living. Enjoy You. Find happiness in the simple moments. Notice the beauty in the world around you. See the love you receive in the eyes of family and friends. Feel the wonderful energy that comes from knowing that you are blessed. Realize this. Recognize this. Acknowledge this. Revel in this. Celebrate you; your life; your gifts.

...OTHERS

This day is new. Treat it as such. See all the possibilities that comes with this and each new day. Bring your energy up and keep it up. Keep it high. Re-establish yourself. Renew yourself. Find yourself again. Encouragement is a powerful gift. It turns negative to positive. It realigns and renews. Be like Johnny Appleseed planting positive thoughts wherever and with whoever you feel needs them. You laugh, but it is so. It is truly needed. Many like you are needed and necessary. The world is in need of your positive influence and light. Just as one candle can be used to light others without diminishing its own light, share your light with the world. Be a beacon for others to follow. Be the sun to brighten their day.

Give of yourself. Allow others to give to you. Allow the exchange. Each will benefit from the gift given by the other. Each will benefit from the gift given of themselves. Lessons are to be learned here. The lesson of giving openly and receiving graciously. The lesson of trusting. The lesson of sharing a part of oneself. The gift of gratitude. It is a gift like no other.

Be the light house that others need to help them find their compass. To see the goal that they seek. Help them find the way through the illusions, see through the fog of self-doubt, falsehoods and untruths of others. Allow your inner light to show; be the beacon that reminds them, that guides them to their own.

Some of the greatest things come from the smallest starts. Each small event, each small gift of positive movement, positive thought adds to the whole. Reality is what you make of it. You can add to the healing energies needed in this world. In many ways you heal others each and every day. A simple smile can start a positive connection. You can soothe another simply with the sound of your voice. The attitude you bring, the poise of your body can heal in ways that you can only start to imagine. Show respect. Show honor. BE an ambassador of love and of light. Like begets like. Embrace the possibilities. What would be the outcome if each person started with something small and simple and inspired another to do the same?

You can touch another's soul without knowing it. Your kindness creates a ripple that brings on more changes for the positive. Little gestures go a very long way in the universe. As you pass one another, choosing to ignore or frown or to simply smile can be the change that turns someone's attitude, and possibly their own sense of self. Keep this in mind. Choose your gestures wisely.

Self-doubt is a small seed that can grow rapidly. There are others around you who hold a poor sense of self. Give them a smile and encouragement. Help them experience new things and maybe their ego will grow just a little. You will find that you have helped heal others and at the same time found healing for yourself.

Your angels and guides are here with you.
We know what you seek. We know you want answers, but they are not for us to give to you. Some things you must learn on your own. Some things are part of the lessons you need to learn. And the things that your heart most wants to hear, you must hear from another. Be true to yourself. Follow your heart, your inner guidance and what you need, what you seek will be found. We know it's hard for you at times to wait, to not know, to be unsure. That in itself is a lesson. Sometimes it's not about you and your comfort. Sometimes it's about another's comfort and concerns.

...RELEASE

Always returning to the same subject. Why is that do you think? Do you really want to return to that situation? Could you trust anyone if you did? Let go of this. It is your past. It no longer exists in your world. Release it so there is room in your life for that which truly matters. Your new life awaits. It truly does. You hold on to sad memories, negative energies. Release them. You will build more, new, happier memories soon.

Emotions, outbursts of emotions, whether tears, anger or both are all a part of healing. Shout if you feel the need to shout. Shake your fists. Scream at the top of your lungs. Revel in the fact that you can. Release is a part of healing. You were given emotions to experience them, not to hide them away, not to block them out. Feel them, use them; experience them. Each feeling, each thought. Go ahead and ask each "why". Shout out each "how come" or "it's not fair". Demand to be heard!! It's ok. It's allowed. It's just a part of who you are. Acknowledge your anger, your frustration. Express your agitation. That is why you are feeling them – to express them. Do not hold on to negativity, but neither should you use negativity to cause harm to others. Simply take the moment in solitude to write out, shout out, scream out or even cry out. To release, to reveal, to resolve the stress you have held inside is more than ok – it is healing. Words that would cause harm or distress to others can be shouted, screamed or simply stated alone, to yourself, to your guides, to your angels. They will understand. They will not take offense; they can be your sounding board when no one else can. Release is exhausting, but it wouldn't be release any other way.

Let go of the everyday world. All matters
will handle themselves. This you know. The
universe works for you, with you. This you also
know. Release the worry for that which is
already solved for you. Release it all for all is
already solved. Be in the now, in this moment
and only this moment. Let the world fall away.
Feel each breath. Slow your rhythm. Nothing
matters but the you that you are now; your
thoughts, your focus, your every sense of
being, right here, right now. Go inside, see
inside. Find the calm that only you can own.
The world around you is but a blur. All that
matters is <u>you</u>. For this moment, this brief,
shining moment find your light. The light within
that starts as a spark, let it glow. Let it grow.
Let it fill you. Feel the power that is you. Feel it

fill every part of your being. Feel it expand out from the physical you, spreading around you, expanding forth, far out into the world. Allow your positive energies to blend with the universe, to add to the collective. Know that you are one with everything, that everything is one with you. Understand that this is so. No matter where you are, no matter what you are doing, universal light and love are yours. Draw from it. Give to it. Share it, as it is meant to be shared.

Your thoughts are scattered. Too many things running through your head to allow you to either focus or drift away into slumber. Why fight what comes to your mind? Allow the thought to appear and then let it fade away. This you should do whatever the thought. They are there for a reason. Accept them, allow them and then let them go. It is much easier when you do. Allow the flow to happen. Let your mind work out all that there is until you see and know what is important. For what is important will show itself once all the random thoughts have moved their way through. Allow the process to happen. Allow the flow to move freely. Soon it will flow easily and freely. Soon the current will take you where you need to go – where it is important to know and to be. You fight much too hard. You try to focus much too hard. You stop the process. You stop whatever may be happening with this trying to freeze, trying to analyze each and every thought. Release. Breathe. Release and let your mind wander. Let all those concerns, worries, random thoughts just flow past the dam that you have constructed. Let them break free. Let yourself break free. Free flowing streams run clear – and you will see that your mind will too once you allow it to happen. Release the stream. Unblock the dam. Let loose the waters. Let the flow begin.

Close your eyes. Take a breath and release. Release all control you feel you must have. Let lose all worries, all concerns, all everything. Let your cares float into the winds. Allow the calmness to wash over you. Allow the river waters to make you clean. The flow of life is there for you. Let it calm you. Let it embrace you. Relax in its waters. Feel the gentle waves, the soft current, just take away all that you need to release. Allow the cleansing waters envelope you and just float as easy as a leaf does along the current. Free and easy. Never fighting, only moving along as the river takes it course. So shall you be. Floating free and easy. Following the flow, trusting the journey.

Center yourself. Breathe. Allow the calm to take over. Release the "what ifs". Release the "how comes". Release all doubts, all questions. Release them all for you already know the answers. There is nothing to fear, nothing to dread, nothing to fixate on. There is only you, only truth, only love. Feel the warmth of that knowledge. Like the warmth of the sun, feel it surround you, fill you, encompass you. You know what is right, what is true, what will be. Deep down, you know these things. Do not create blocks, problems, worries that do not exist, that are not needed. Open your heart. Open your mind. Open your soul to the positive energies that are always yours to claim. Feel at peace. Be at peace. BE peace itself. You are loved. You are love. BE Love. Be Joy. Be Happiness. Be all and everything you wish in your life. It is yours to claim. It is yours to enjoy. It is yours already. It is yours now, at this very moment. Allow it, Claim it. BE it.

Your crying is done. No more tears, no more sorrow, only happy times ahead. The only tears you will be shedding are those of joy. Can you feel the lightness around you? That heavy cloud is gone is it not? Yes my dear, you have something special coming your way. So don't over think, don't dwell and worry, just smile and know it's on its way. Because it is.

Your mind is mixed. Thoughts intermingle and you do not know which way to turn or what to concentrate on. This is ok. It's part of your growing, part of the sorting of your life. New beginnings are coming. Old knowledge, old manners are being released. It is normal. It is good. Emotions are played out and finally their grasp over you released. You feel deeply, although you try to hide this from everyone. Deep emotions take a while to work themselves through, to work out. Honor yourself. Honor your thoughts and feelings. Acknowledge that they once were. Acknowledge that they are no longer part of your life and release them as they need to be released. Make room for new emotions, new memories, new events. Clear the path. Clear the way. New paper. New page. New start. New songs to sing. New dances to dance. New smiles. New life. Allow the flow to move you to where you need to be. Remember how a leaf floats easily on top of the water. Enjoy the ride. Your sun is shining. Relax. We have everything covered. Let us take care of you. Ride along for this part of your journey. Relax. Nothing more.

Don't fight the tears. Let them flow. Let them release what needs to be released. Let them wash away what needs to be washed away. Then when you are done, when you are all cried out, acknowledge them. Acknowledge the release and prepare to smile again.

Let go of the anger and frustration. Do not allow it to fester in you. Start to release. It is good that you recognize your feelings and can concentrate on letting them go. Do not talk to others about things now. Wait until you have released all and you have achieved a calmer state.

Many thoughts run through your mind.
Happy thoughts, sad thoughts, thoughts of hope, thoughts of regret. Thoughts of possibilities, thoughts of definite loss. Many thoughts indeed. Tears flow with emotions. Memories filled by song. Regrets energized by lyrics from another life. You were sad, yes, but it was good to release that energy. Sometimes letting go is braver than holding on. Acknowledging and accepting your emotions is a truly brave act. Letting them run their course takes skill and knowledge. Your tears are gone and those emotions no longer have a place in your life. Letting them go, letting them flow was a very good thing, better than you ever can imagine. You have lowered the blocks that were in your way. Opening the floodgates relieved the pressure, lowered the levels so that others may cross. Let go of your past. Those defining moments are done. They have served their purpose and now it is time to reap the bounties of all those past choices, decisions, and lessons.

Releasing energies is good. Especially those you didn't realize you were still holding on to. You will find that you are able to do this more and more often. All is good. Recycling, transforming energies, releasing and renewing is always good. Honor the release. Honor the feelings, the emotions and energies surrounding what you are releasing. Acknowledge that they were important to your life at one time and that they served their purpose well. But now is a time for letting go and moving on. At time for growth and renewal. As you are releasing energies also remember to release your heart. It has been burdened for far too long. The words will come. The moment will be right and you will know exactly what to say and what to do. Your higher self knows and will take over. Trust in yourself and you will know the way.

Let go, release it all. Allow your light to shine once more. Far too long have you cried in the shadows. Far too long have you cried for far too long. Brilliant things are meant for you. Your light must shine so they will find their way to you. End this now. Sulk no more. Pine no more. Smile again. Live again. BE again. It is time. Time to live the life you were always meant to know. Out amongst the world. Not closed inside this cave you have built. Share yourself with others. Allow the light that radiates from you be seen by others around you. Heal yourself this way. I know disappointment has been along your path. It has been for others as well. But those are only stepping stones to walk upon, not be buried under. Get out. Walk from this darkness you have allowed yourself. This anger is not yours. Do not embrace it any longer. Ask for healing and it shall be granted. We are gathered here to help. We are ready for your call. Ask. Just ask.

The storms have passed. The storms your soul has gone through are over. The calm has arrived. Brighter days, better skies, better attitudes, openness to new thing arriving. All is good. It will happen, the life your wish for will be yours. Just know it will. Don't worry about the how's, the where's, the when's. Know it is to be. It is not too much to ask for, to dream for, for it is already yours and is on its way. Follow your heart. Allow yourself the freedom to dream, to reach out, to connect with the universe and its energies. You will know the way. You will know without asking what to do. You should know it will happen. The number of days until it arrives is not important. It will happen. Release the doubt and the worry.

Breathe. Relax. Allow it to happen as you should allow everything to happen. On its own, naturally. Without control. Without worry. Let yourself go. Let all come to you as it should. No worry for protection. We are here. We will provide that. No harm will come to you, rest assured. Release the fear that you have built up in your mind. God is with you always. We are with you always. Relax your fears. Relax your fingers. Release your grip for there is no need to cling to control. Trust. Believe. All is taken care of. All that is needed will be provided. This you should know. Believe this in all things. It works on all levels for all needs and desires. Remove your doubts. Remove the blocks you have built or re-built. Feel the release. Feel the energy flowing freely once again. Allow the positive currents to move through your life. Sail along this river and enjoy the ride. It is time to believe again. It is time to allow again. It is time. Know this – it is time.

Release the darkness, the fog that you have pulled around you. It is not the protective blanket you thought you have covered yourself with. It is a shroud of heavy energy that will not protect you, but will smother you as it does not allow the light within to shine forth. You are a child of light. You are a child of God. Bring forth the light that you have hidden away for far too long. Allow the goodness that is in you, that IS you to shine forth. Mistakes have been made, yes, but mistakes were to serve as lessons in your path only, not to last as punishments throughout your life, throughout your existence. You have asked for forgiveness from others and forgiveness from God. Now it the time to grant forgiveness to yourself. Do this now. Do this today. Shed that weight, that heavy-ness before it consumes you. Know that your light is much more powerful than anything that may come your way. Embrace your light, allow it to embrace you. You have a bright future ahead if you only allow it to happen.

You are at the threshold of change. Many new things. Many new experiences are awaiting you. You have your hand on the door knob. Just open the door and step through. There is no need to allow just one aspect of your life to hold you back, to keep you from the other things that are just as important to your path. One piece will tie in with the other. One part will shine light, will bring focus to the other. All are necessary. All are entwined. You will see the connection once you let go of the fear.

It is time to let go. Let go of whatever you have been holding onto. Make room for new changes. Make way for new energies. Make a place for new choices.

What do you fear? Truly? And why is there so much of it? There is such a bright future ahead, yet you cover it with the cloak of despair that you cling to so tightly. Do you not believe that good is yours to claim and is coming your way? You are powerful, you know what others do not, yet you cannot grasp this for yourself? Silly child. Smile, be happy. Bring the energies of love and light to you, forgo those thoughts that perpetuate the negative. You are a beacon of light. Be that beacon. Do not allow the fog of confusion and worry dull the brightness that is you. You and only you have the power to determine your day. Begin to influence others and stop letting others influence you. Stand tall. Stand bright. Let the light of you shine through.

You know your heart. You know your truths. Do not worry. Do not rely on others to bring this to you. You are all you truly need. We know you are afraid to hope. Afraid to let go and dream. We understand that you have been here before and tricked before into beliefs that were never entirely true. Release the fear. Release that worry, that doubt, that anxiety. They serve you no longer because they are no longer true. All is yours if you just believe. All is yours if you just release yourself and allow it to finally happen and come to you with no conditions, no restrictions. With free will and open arms, don't try to control this. You no longer need to protect yourself this way. Trust yourself. Trust in your heart. Unlock those chains. Release the grip you have held for so long. Allow yourself that freedom.

You have asked for release. And it is done. Your life will begin new from this moment on. Can you feel the clearing; the lifting of the shadow; of weight? Can you feel the lightness returning? Can you feel the renewed energy coming to you? You have finally broken through that wall of sadness. Darkness is fading away. The light, the power, the strength is there once more. Time to move forward as only you can.

...LESSONS

This is a time of growth for you. Not a lesson of patience, but one of trust. Trust in yourself. Trust in your knowledge. Trust in your worth and what you know is right. Trust in who you are, in what you are. No one knows this better than you. No matter what is around you. No matter what influences are involved, you are the constant. Remain constant. Keeping true to yourself will be the biggest reward. Do not waver from the path you have chosen; the stance you have decided to make for you made it with your greatest good in mind. It remains constant as well. Your greatest good is always a constant. Little things such as this, brief moments are all that they are. Remaining true will have the biggest payoff in the end. Do not cheapen yourself with concessions, with indiscretions that may serve the moment or the ego. That is not the prize you seek. You are a prize worth waiting for. Hold fast. Hold strong, even though others around you do not. Their choice, their path is their own. What is right for them is not right for you.

Holding true to yourself is the greatest lesson you can learn. Many will come and go trying to test your resolve. Trying to change your mind or at least make you forget yourself for just a moment. That is only because they are looking for who they are and have not yet found themselves. Those who know who they are, what they believe in, do not try to force their beliefs on others. They do not try to change others to fit into their personal picture. Do not believe them when they tell you that you are alone, that others like you do not exist. That is only to scare you into fitting into their cloud, their picture of what should be. Hold true and you will see. Hold true and you will find. Know yourself. Be yourself. What you need, what you desire will be yours if you keep that picture clear.

You can teach and be taught your own lesson at the same time. Learn from the lessons you teach others. Every teacher is a student. Every student is a teacher. They are one and the same. A balance, a sharing of energies. Growth brought forth from the connection of mind and spirit.

Lessons and healings take several forms and are delivered in many different ways. But they are lessons and healings none the less. Sometimes they are for others. Sometimes there for you. Sometimes they are for both.

It is okay and will be okay. This is a step. You know that and have always anticipated it coming. There is no intentional harm. It is nothing personal, and what you have asked for. It is all good. It is a part of the flow of life. Remind yourself of that when the time comes.

No harm, no foul. It is not personal. It is just the circle of life. The way we are to evolve and grow. It is good. Even sorrow in tears are good. It reminds you that you are alive that you are feeling emotions.

Know that greater things are to come, but do not let that trick you, lead you to try to rush through the steps you must take. And take the steps you must. It will not take long. You will master each one easily and quickly. Know this and be confident of your talents. Do not question. Do not doubt or second guess and you will move along as you should. Just know that you have a purpose and that you are fulfilling that purpose with each day, with each lesson, with each breath, with each thought, each step. You are one with the universe. One with the highest power, the highest good. You are a child of light. Behold all that you are and all that you will be.

Guides, helpers, come and go as you need them. One you have accomplished something, gained a talent, achieved a necessary part of your life, they move on. And a new guide, a new helper will appear to help you with that which is lacking or needs adjustment. It is a good thing when they go – it means that you – both of you, you and helper alike have done what was needed and are ready to move on to the next lesson.

There will be others to come into your life. Others for you to make a difference in their life and for them to touch yours. Some will come and your path will merge and become one. Others will parallel your path and cross only briefly. Each contact has a purpose. Each a part of the plan. Learn from them as they will learn from you. Honor the part they play, the part you play in each other's life. That is your true path. That is your true purpose.

...*LOVE*

Trust your heart. Trust yourself, your true feelings. Know yourself and your needs, your desires. Another lesson, yes. More definement. More definition. What is it you want – truly want? Why would you settle for less? Part of the package is still not the package. Is just a taste enough to satisfy your hunger? Honor yourself. Honor your dreams and your desires for the best that can be. Is this truly the best?

Breathe, above all breathe. Take in each moment as it comes. Breathe with each moment. Sense yourself, your being, your inner being breathing. Sense the pulse, the rhythm, and know its truth. Know your truth. See the beauty beyond your eyes, see the beauty within the soul. Know the seed of love in all that is waiting to spring forth and grow. Some keep it hidden, afraid to let it loose and wander through this world. Others share their love freely, openly, much more quickly than others deem appropriate. Who has the right to judge? The importance is <u>not</u> in how quickly the love is being shared, but that <u>it is</u> being shared in the first place. Do not hoard what is meant to be shared or what grows with each sharing. Do not hide the light, the love that was placed inside you, for you by faith, to let it be known by all around you. Share your love and others will share theirs just as equally. Yes, there will be those who cling tightly to that kernel terrified of what may happen if they loosen their grip. But love them none the less, and for this reason, love them all the more. When they realize that there is more love for them than what they hold close, they will loosen their fingers and allow themselves to reach for more and in that reaching, will learn, will know that their original seed has tripled itself in the reaching, in the sharing that comes when release is allowed. Giving out and returning back as easy as breathing. Share your love even with, especially with, those who aren't ready to do so themselves. One breath at a time. One heart at a time.

It may take time. But in the scheme of things, all you have is time. Time is infinite, time is the one thing that everyone possesses. Whether it is squandered or cherished, everyone has time. Live in each moment, make each moment last. Fill each one with wonder, with awe, with joy, with sorrow, with laughter, with love. It matters not as long as you live in the moment and make each moment as full as the last. Be. Be as best you can, as much as you can. Feel, sense, experience as much as possible each and every moment you exist. For you do exist. Stop worrying about what ifs. Stop holding on to your heart like it needs so much protection. You were given a heart to use, to share, to feel, to express. To BE. Unwrap your heart. Remove that protective barrier. It is not necessary. It is not how one heals. No different than an athlete's injury – you must use and re-use the muscle to maintain, to regain and increase strength. This is how it is with your heart as well. You cannot live protected. You cannot live without feeling, without emotion, without reaching out to others for that connection, for that completion once the connection is made. True, not all loves last forever. But all love is worth the time that it lasts. It is a necessary part of the human condition, the human connection.

All will be well. All will follow according to the plan that has been set by you, for you. Feel the rhythm. Feel the beating of its drum. Your heart is calling to be heard. Listen. Listen well for it tells no lies. Listen for the truth of the heart for it is your connection to the universe, your connection to your true spirit. Live by that rhythm, follow the pulse it sends you, for it is your truest self, speaking in a language that only you can hear, only you can honor.

Believe that love will come your way. The right love. The best love is yours. Go ahead, sing your love songs. Write your love poems. Dream your dreams. Feel that it is with you already because it already is. Sense it. Experience it. Send those energies out into the world, into the universe. Send the vibrations out to the one that will be searching for its match. Just know it to be out there. Know that will arrive, will grow at its own rate, in its own time, but that it will arrive.

There are many things you should already know - but you seem to have forgotten. You are beautiful, you are blessed, you <u>are</u> desirable. Not everyone will see that, but that is ok- you are not meant to be for everyone. Only a few will see you in your true beauty. Only a few will see the fabulous light that shines from you. The others are not worthy. The one, the true one will find you.

Everyone has barriers. You have barriers of your own as well. Are the ones you have constructed permanent? Are they valid? Are they true? Are they necessary? Protection- that is something that everyone seeks. A need that everyone shares. You must realize this. You must honor this. Release is the hardest of things to do – and the greatest gift that anyone can give. To trust enough to release that grasp, to let go of that fear, is the bravest, most honorable thing one can do. Letting go of that protection. Lowering that guard. Putting away that shield is a selfless act – and one not often come by. It is a gift that must be honored, cherished, acknowledged and held in high respect. It is an honor to receive that kind of trust and not to be taken lightly. Remember this always. Remember this especially when the time comes for barriers to fall.

Wanting what you desire is not a bad thing at all. All of humankind desires as such. It is in your nature. It is how you are made. Each seeking companionship, partnership, tenderness, love, sharing – it is the best part of being human. We do not think that you are wrong to do so. We only wish that you do not forgo all other happiness because of the lack of this one. You have much to be happy about. You are blessed in many, many ways and you will be blessed in many more to come. You have a wonderful heart. Do not shield it. Do not hide it. Do not shut it down. Let it glow, let it burn brightly. Let the inner light that is you shine so beautifully. Believe us when we tell you that this is temporary. Your tears, your fears are just temporary. You will know great joy!

I know it's hard to believe, you have been hurt so many times before. You have built that wall so damn high. A wall not of brick, but of a belief in the lie that you are not good enough, that you will never find love. Tear down that wall, knock it down, climb over it, go around it. BUILD A BRIDGE and GET OVER IT. Release your fears once and for all. You are meant for a fine, true, rich love. Open your heart and keep it open. Don't close it up again. Remain open. Remain free to receive. Don't force it. It will happen openly and on its own.

Be yourself, allow your love and energy to shine. Only this will attract the love you seek. Prepare for your partner. Maintain the right mind set. Keep preparing. Keep believing. Keep smiling and sending your positive energy out into the universe. Love will find you. Like a moth to a flame, your energy will attract your partner's. Know that when the time is right, you will find each other.

Do not allow yourself to be discouraged.

Hold on to your belief in all things possible. It is what makes you who you are. Looking for the positive, for the possible is key to you and your sense of self. It will be one of the things others will find most charming about you. Your energy is of light, of hope and love. All of things are possible in your world, your eye, your heart. Hope is alive in you. Love is alive in you. Do not let that go. There IS magic. It is in you and others like you. You are infectious. Your smile, the twinkle in your eye, your laugh is infectious. And is needed now more than ever. Your openness to possibility keeps the door open to hope and light. Too many have closed the door. Too many have given up hope and lost their hearts to closed minds, closed places. Your heart flows free with love, hope and possibilities. You love quickly and easily because you love openly and freely. Not many can. Many more should. Love well. Love fully. Love openly as only you can. It is a blessing; to be loved as you love. Few understand or know its true value. But those that do will treasure it forever.

You have the answers they are there within you, although you might not find them or even want to hear them. You're not alone even if you forget that from time to time. Someone is always with you. You have pulled yourself into that circle where being alone is all you have come to expect, so that is what you were given. You love guardedly. You participate guardedly. You prepare yourself for them to leave and they will because you set yourself for that. How can you break that cycle? Love freely, completely, expect nothing. Enjoy what you have fully and completely. They haven't abandoned you the are just moving to another place on their path and you must move to another place on yours.

Do not be deceived by wanderlust. Do not allow yourself to falter in your path on your quest. Keep moving forward. Ask for clarity. Listen with your heart, your soul, your higher self. You will know the truth. You will need to remember this when those who want to deceive you for their own means come to call. Do not believe big stories. The bigger the story the larger the lie. There are those that cannot be trusted. Do not allow your heart to set itself up for yet another fall.

We know — we truly do. We wish we could wipe away your tears, ease your pain and suffering. Fill that void you seem to have. But we cannot. Others love you, you know that. You <u>are </u>loved. Not just by one, but by many. We are always with you. You are never alone. We realize that it is not the type of companionship you desire, that you long for, but it is real and it is yours. Believe in yourself as we do. Trust in your heart as we know it to be true. You will find what you desire. Know that others care and love you. Let that fill you. Let that warm you like arms around you in a hug. Love will be there for you. Your time for love is on its way. You will be surprised that you ever doubted its coming.

...STRENGTH

Don't give up. Don't give in to this feeling that creeps back at you. You are stronger than this. This is all temporary. Your life is about to take a turn for the better. This is right for you. Do not doubt that for a minute. Things will turn, your life is blessed by God. Better health. Better wealth. Better home. Better love. Much more happiness. Fight this darkness. Believe you are blessed because you are.

What do you search for? You seem to have questions but you cannot find the words. Something is troubling you. Something just doesn't seem right, does it? Many changes are coming, but you have known this for a while. You will not find an answer if you do not ask. You cannot ask what you do not know. Where is the key that you seem to be looking for? The key to unlock whatever it is you feel has been holding you back? What has been holding you back? No one, nothing, but yourself.

Gather your strength. Gather your wits. Calm your mind. Ease your soul. Ease your spirit. All is well and always has been. All is working as it should, as it will for your greatest good. Your heart knows this, even though your mind may have forgotten. Your heart remembers. Listen to your heart, not your head. Feel the calm that comes from knowing with the heart. Feel the serenity, the balance that always exists inside you, is always there for you to find if you just search with your heart. You are connected as all beings are. You will always find yourself where you are supposed to be while traveling down your path. Your heart is your compass in all things. Follow your heart, for your truth is there.

Keep your focus. Keep your faith. Keep your belief alive. It is not over. It has only just begun. Wonderful things are just beginning for you. Do not panic that the start is slower than you wish. In truth, it is not slow at all. It is how it should be, must be. Believe. Know. Grow. As with all things in life, there is a lesson here as well. All in its time. Honor the pace. Honor the process. Trust that you will find the way. Acknowledge what you are feeling. Explore the emotions, then release them and move on. Hold true to the positive, pure energies. Express the negative. Acknowledge that they have occurred. Then let them go, for they are just a part of the process, part of defining who you are, what you want, where you want to go, where you want to be. You know this. Let it happen for you.

We wish that things had worked
more smoothly than they have throughout your life. But there were lessons to be learned and things needed to bring you where you are right now.

You are such a great spirit. You are strong and powerful. Yet in this human form you find yourself weak, defeated and crying so often. It is so sad, so hard to watch. It is a shame you cannot remember just how powerful you are. How much vital energy you give off.

What do you wish for? What do you seek most? Love? Acceptance? Validation? All are yours already. Your life is not as empty as you seem to think. <u>Love</u> is all around you. Friends, family, you are loved. <u>Acceptance</u> is yours as well. You are welcomed wherever you go. People look forward to seeing you, greeting you, speaking with you. <u>Validation</u>? What more do you need than what you have just received? You do matter. Your existence does count. You can hear the voices of your friends, your true friends – they know you matter. Go. Live. Do. Experience life. Fill your time with fun, with laughter. Do not allow yourself to wallow in the emptiness that you have created for yourself. For it is just an illusion. Your life, your soul – you – are filled with light and love. You just need to remember that. Celebrate that. Live that.

Heed your own voice. Follow the path meant for you. You are growing. Growing, changing, deciding exactly who you are and what you want to be. Growth is not exclusive to the young. Growing takes place at all times of life. No matter what your path. No matter where you are on that path. It took all this time to realize just who you are and how wonderful you have become. Your life was a gift of lessons, of becoming, of growing and of realization. Celebrate who you are. Feel the power of that knowledge, that sense of self.

Do not worry, this phase will end for you soon. It is only an adjustment period. Time for things to come to a close. Time for thing to start anew. Adjusting energies, wave lengths, focuses. Do not worry, these feelings will not last long. This non-feeling, as you describe it, will not last long. You will begin to feel like yourself again. You will feel alive again. Your batteries just needed recharging, not everyone can be ON all the time. Not even you.

We could make you false promises. But what good would it do? You would get excited and then angry when they did not happen. You have asked us to provide you with the truth and the truth alone. So that is what we are trying to do. There are many good things in store for you. But now is a time of focus, a time of quiet. Like winter before the spring and its flowers. Yes, we know you hate winter, but it is necessary just as this is necessary. Reflect on your blessings that you can and have acknowledged. Understand that. Then acknowledge where those come from.

This is not your time. We know it is hard for you, but it is not yet your time. When it arrives, it will be grand and glorious. But until then, you must stay strong in your belief.

Do not give into the darkness that you feel gathering around you. It is but a fleeting moment in time. Fleeting – that is all it is. Know that you are never alone. Know that you are loved. We wish that things would have worked more smoothly than they have. Throughout your life. But there were lessons to learn and things needed to bring you where you are right now. We know it has been hard at times. We know it is hard at this moment. We feel your pain, your sorrow. We see your tears, they are but temporary. Believe that. You will laugh again. You will smile again. You will be happy once more. The next set of tears that fall will be those of joy. If you don't believe anything else- Believe this – you ARE loved.

You have given up, stopped the search – at least you say you have. "Tired of trying", you say. Maybe that is for the best. Maybe the trying is what held you back in the first place. You know sometimes one can try too hard. Maybe that is the case with you? Do not over extend. Just be. Just breathe and be the wonderful person that you are. In itself, that is a blessing.

Allow yourself to breathe. Do not give in to the shadows that you feel surrounding you. Do not confuse boredom with sadness. Do not take on emotions that are not there or that are not yours to take on. Honor yourself above all. Be true to your heart. Know your heart. Know what is of you and you alone.

Your strength is returning. You will feel it more and more each day. Happiness will find you again. You will feel complete and clear once more. This process is over. Your metamorphosis is complete. The process has ended. It was painful, but necessary. You had to lose everything to gain so much more. You had to release. You had to relinquish all that you had. Starting over. Starting revived, refreshed. Reboot as you would say for computers. That was needed. Pain is never something we wish on anyone, but sometimes it takes that to get to where you need to be. You are where you need to be. Here. Now. This exact moment. Not anticipating. Not planning. And yes, not knowing. Allow what must happen to happen. Allow the process to unfold. Know that when the time is right, all will fall into place. Your eyes will sparkle again. You will smile again.

You sense many things. You sense much turmoil. But this is not for you, it is only in the space that you inhabit at the moment. Do not try to take it in or claim it. It is not yours to claim. It is a message for you to realize the experiences of others. Stay outside of it. Do not allow it to take a space in your heart or in your soul. You have much more important work to do. That negativity is beneath you and you are so far beyond that now. You have the tools that you need to protect yourself; to shield yourself from the negativity of others. You are such a powerful, talented soul. Believe in yourself. Believe in your strengths, your inner wisdom. You have allies that are equally strong. Connect with them. Interact with them on a level that only you will understand. You will draw strength from that level of camaraderie, of friendship, of kin ship. For you are family you are connected on several planes of reality. You know this. You have felt this before. Call upon those of your kind, your kin, your tribe, your clan. Feed the power in that connection. That will get you through.

...FAITH

Take that leap of faith and you will realize it was only one simple step and not a dive over a bottomless cavern after-all.

Many messages are coming to you. Many thoughts run through your mind. Which one thought will serve you now? Let go and let God. But you already know that, so you say. Others have told you to create your destiny. Which is the one to listen to? Which is the one that is right? Maybe it's both. Create and then let go or let go and then create. Either way you are blessed.

You must have faith. You must hold on to that faith. Believe and it shall be. Do not worry about the venue. You will be guided to be where you need to be and when you need to be there. For whatever event that needs to happen.

Do no more. Hurt no more. Just go about your day and just by knowing that what you seek is there for you, and the universe will place it in your path. Allow the daily life to happen. Because it will come if you let it but only if you let it. You are the powerful creator, do not forge, do not bring forth blocks or walls by focusing on doubt. The universe is bringing you all that you need, all that you focus on. If you focus on worry, on lack, you will continue to worry, continue to see lack. Know that what you need will be there for you when you need it. It will appear. You have asked. You shall receive, first-class delivery every time.

The universe knows what it is doing

– even if you do not.

I see, you've been thinking again, haven't you? That's not always a good thing for you. You tend to over think when you have time on your hands. Well, relax. It's all under control. Give it over to the universe to help you through this. To set things right. Just relax and know that you will have your answer soon, that is what you asked for isn't it? There isn't anything you can do. Nothing you should do, but relax and know that the universe will provide the answer for you, one way or another. So, either it will happen, or it won't. If it does, wonderful, you can start fresh and see where things go. If it doesn't, then not much has changed from what you were already used to, but you can begin a new life and move forward. It is all good.

We are excited. We are celebrating already. Can you feel us laughing, cheering, smiling? How wonderful it will be! How wonderful is. Know that it will happen. Know that it is there for you and it will be. And it is yours. Reach out your hand and grab that brass ring. It is within your reach and is yours to claim. Who needs a lottery ticket with wonderful life that is yours to own.

You ask questions, but are you prepared for the answers? You must wait. As hard as it is, you must wait. Do not hold your life in place. Do not put a hold on your life. Live it as full as you can, as you will. But you must wait for the time to be right for what you truly seek. It will come. It will be yours. But it will only come as it will. Nothing you can do will change that.

You are letting details get in your way.

Why do you worry so about silly things? You know that God has a plan for you and you will be given all that you need to make that plan succeed. Feel the strength that is inside you. That has been given to you. Know that you have a connection with the universe that few have experienced. Your time is coming, in truth, it has already arrived, you just need to slow down and let it reveal itself to you.

Follow your heart. You know what must be done, what is needed and how to proceed. Guidance will be yours. Assistance will be yours. You just need to ask. But you will need little outside guidance as you will know intuitively what to do. You are in tune with what is needed and when the time arrives, you will be ready.

Today you asked for help. Know that you have been heard and your prayers will be answered. It is hard for you to admit that you need help, we know this. But there are points in your life when you must reach out to a higher power to move forward- and you have done exactly that. You felt the change, you felt things lighten did you not? Rejoice for you have been heard. Know that this is true. Hold on to your dreams for they are about to come true.

Why do you think the way you do? Do you have no faith? Do you not remember the good things that you have already received? Blessings come in many shapes and are delivered in many ways. Not all have pretty bows, not all are supposed to. Some come in the simple and quite moments. Others come in loud blustering storms. Look around with renewed vision. Find the blessings that were yours today. The more you find, the more you will see.

Belief, trust, faith and understanding
are all key, all important. All must BE in order
for you to have what you desire most. Re-align
yourself, your energies, your faith and belief in
everything to make things work for your
greater good once more.

You have been waiting, haven't you?

Waiting for messages. Waiting for love. Waiting for life. Waiting. Just Waiting. Time moves and you feel you have not. So much has changed yet so little as well. Funny how perception works, is it not? You ask for knowledge. You ask for information, yet when it is given, you question. You wonder. You worry about the outcome, about the truth of what you have been told. Silly goose, you shall see. You shall know all there is to know, all there is to see. Validation will be yours. So much sooner than you can imagine.

...BE CALM

Quiet your mind. Slow your breath.

Ease into this meditation. Open to receive the knowledge to be given to you. No need to rush, the flow is within you, within us. We are one and there is no need to hurry along, no need to rush the process. Breathe. Breathe deeply, once again. We know how much you need to slow down. How important it is for you to be calm, relaxed. No need to hurry, we have an infinite amount of time. We always have – you always have. Live in this moment of infinite moments.

Swirling, whirling, thoughts spin, wind and twirl within your mind. Relax, let them go - let them calm, let them slow and fall down. Quietly, like the leaves of autumn. See them drift, floating, falling gracefully, quietly to the ground. Quiet your mind. Allow the peace within. Allow the silence to take over. Pause, breathe, if only for a moment. Stay in that moment. Hold time still. Hold your mind still. In the silence you will find your answers. In the quiet, in the calm, the truth will come. Know this above all, trust yourself, you already know the answers. You just need to take the time to listen. Listen to the quiet voice within. The language only you can hear, only you can understand. Feel it drawing near, feel the knowledge coming closer. Let it unfold as it will. Do not rush. Do not challenge. Do not doubt, above all do not question what you know for you have the knowing. You have had it all along. You just forgot that you did. Now is the time to remember. Now is the time to restore the knowledge you've hidden away for far too long. Allow it to come forth, allow it to move freely, openly without shackles, without barriers, without fear. Open it as easily as you do a book. You will find the pages you need as you need them. The answers are there. You only need to ask and look inside.

So many questions running through your head. So many, it's hard for you to choose which one to ask. Maybe, you shouldn't ask any. Just be, just breathe, let them settle down, let them place themselves in their own order. They will, you know, if you just let them. When the time is right, when you need to know, it will be there for you. The answers to your questions will come, they always have.

What do you seek? What do you want to know? Go inside yourself for the answers. Allow the wisdom to rise. Allow your inner light to shine. It is there for you. All answers are there for you. Breathe. Breathe again. Slow yourself. Calm yourself. Focus yourself. Ask and it shall be answered. Believe the truth that is you. What you need to hear will come to you. Allow it to flow. Allow it to rise to the surface.

Many thoughts are rushing through
your head. What should I do? When should I
do? Who? What? When? Where? Why? All are
questions that your ego is asking. What are the
answers your heart is bringing? Those are the
thoughts you should pay attention to. Your
heart knows, your higher self knows. You truly
know. What lies ahead, lies ahead. It is good
and as it should be. That is not what you should
focus on now. Now is where your focus should
stay. Be in the now. For this is where you are
at the moment. The future will take care of
itself. It is for you to take care of the you that
you are now. Be in the moment and hear your
heart as it is in this moment. Turn off the
clutter. Turn off the noise. Listen to that voice
that tiny voice inside. It whispers the truth that
only you can hear. Be truthful to yourself.

Relax, enjoy, take it easy. Allow the day to flow as it will, as it should. Do not over think. Do not over plan. All will fall into place. For you as it always does. Relax. Let the flow happen. No worries. No plans. No expectations. Live in the moment. Enjoy the moments as they come. You can do that can't you? Do not try to think things out. Do not pull apart the pieces and examine each under a microscope. Do not worry about the details. They will take care of themselves. Today just flow. Dance to the music that is today. Sing today's song.

Try to connect with your higher self. Work past the noise, past the fog, past all that seems to block you. Connect for you can and you will. It is part of you. That even you cannot deny. Yes, it has been hard. Yes, there have been blocks along the way, but it is all part of your path... Good, bad, easy, hard, it is all part of the plan, and part of life. We know your disappointment. We know your frustration. We even understand what is happening with you today. All for a reason. All for a purpose. All for the plan. Let go. Allow. Let the path flow as it happens, as it may. Do you really need control? Do you really need to know every detail? Be happy knowing the result. Know it will happen. The details are unimportant. Let the surprise come and enjoy it when it does. How uninteresting life would be if you have already read the script? Enjoy the precious moments as they unfold. Life should be an adventure, a new and exciting adventure every day. Each new day, a brand-new adventure. Open up to the undefined. Open up to all of the possibilities in store for you. Allow the flow. Ride along and enjoy the trip. Do not splash. Do not struggle and fight the current. Do not try to paddle. We are your safety net. Your greatest good is the tie line. So. relax and enjoy the ride.

All is finally re-aligning itself for you, for your life. Dis-chord was all around you. (And you felt it.) To reclaim your life, your power was needed. It was all that was needed. No longer at odds with your thoughts or your messages. Your mind is no longer scrambled. Continue on this path. Remember to take time alone. To breathe deep. To be quiet and to meditate. Allow time for yourself. You know you can do this. You will not lose precious time, but will gain solidness and strength. Which is a treasure and a blessing beyond measure.

Meditation is different for everyone. Some sit in a quiet room, some write thoughts and ideas brought to them while others chant and use rhythmic movements and celebrate with song. All is good, all is necessary. But each must find their own. None is better than the other. Each must find their own way for their own path, their own pattern.

Settle in. Let yourself breathe and let go. You are safe. It will remain so. Allow the quiet within take over.   Feel the rhythm, feel the energy of nature, of mother earth. Allow the world beyond that float away, dissolve from your awareness. Hear the call of the cicadas. Let them become your white noise. Let them cloak all surrounding influences, interruptions. Focus on this message and only this message. Trust. Trust in your gifts, your talents, your abilities. Trust in yourself.

What do you seek? Answers? Questions? Encouragement? New information? So many possibilities. So many new chances. So many changes on their way. How will you know what to watch for? You will know. This is true. Relax and let it happen. Keep your mind set at ease to bring it all along.

Take this time to rejuvenate, to relax, to pull yourself out of the system. Just focus on yourself, your surroundings, your space in all its forms. Stop thinking so much, stop forcing things to come to your mind. You are only creating blocks- the blocks you have been trying to avoid. A light will come, knowing will be gained, shared, formed. This time is to stay neutral. Not to rev energies, or slam to a stop. Be neutral. Be still. Allow. Accept and you shall receive and we will be there to celebrate when you do.

Feel the calm. Know the rightness that is you. Body, mind and spirit are all connected, all integrated. This is good, this is how it is meant to be. Be mindful of that connection. Sense the integration. For in that integration is the one-ness that you seek.

Today should be a time of reflection.
Travel nowhere except in your mind. Be within yourself today. Hear the little voices that call to you. Let your memories go where they may for they are meant to serve you today. As you open your heart, so should you open your mind. Both are needed to open the path to allow what is to come. Sit here, be here, allow the thoughts, the music, the stories to unfold as they may. Open your heart to receive, open your mind to see. Body, mind and spirit are all connected. Allow; breathe; allow some more. Do not try to control your thoughts. Do not try to make them happen. They will as they may. Just allow, accept and experience.

Breathe deep. Breathe in deeply and slowly. Calm your mind. Calm your heart. Calm your soul. Listen to the world around you. Release your inner calm. Let it take over, let it wash over you and your consciousness. Restore yourself. Renew yourself. Take this moment, this very moment for you and only you. Hear your breathing. Concentrate on that alone. Feel your inner calm wafting, floating out from within. This is where you need to be. With yourself. In yourself. About yourself. This is where you must be. The You, you must be. The You that you were meant to find. To find this, you need no one but yourself. Feel the peace. Find the center. Find the magic that is you. Find the love that fills the sense of self, the love that surrounds you. Yes. Now you know.

Clear your mind of all those questions.
You have too many to keep track of – too many
to focus on all at once. Clear your mind.
Breathe for a minute or two. Nothing more,
just breathe. Your answers are coming. You
will know what you need to know when you
need to know it. Trust that. Trust in yourself
most of all.

Relax, no stress, no worry, only light
and love should fill your soul, your mind. This is good. This is how is should be and will be. Feel the warmth – like that of the sun shining on your face. Feel it soothe. Feel it caress. This is where you should go, this is how you should feel, relaxed, at ease. Think of this, remember this, use this moment whenever you need to. Quiet moment, gentle, relaxing, carefree moment.

...INNER WISDOM

So many questions – and for you,

not enough answers. Do not doubt what you have been given. You know the truth. Just because it is pleasing to hear, does not make it wrong. Sometimes good news, happy news is just that. Accept and allow all that is good, all that is happy. Do not over-think. Do not worry. Do not analyze. That only interrupts the flow. Accept what you see, hear, feel. The affirmations, the confirmations are coming. Know this. Watch for them and they will arrive. Expect them to be delivered and delivered they will be. Like any blessing, faith, true faith is required. Feel it be yours, picture it already in your heart, in your hand, in your soul and you shall have whatever that may be. Worry not. Fret not. Do believe it is yours, just as you have imagined.

Clear your mind. Clear your thoughts.
Release all those you do not wish to
contemplate at this time. Allow only those
messages to flow that are of your highest
good. Connect with yourself. Connect with the
universe. Connect. Simply connect. Feel the
energies around you. Feel the information that
is being brought forward. Do not think. Do not
analyze. Just receive. Give greetings to all, all
thoughts, all feelings and images that flow
from your higher self for your greater good.
Allow the thoughts, the messages to flow and
they will flow easily. Your inner wisdom will
bring the information you need the most.

Believe in yourself. Do not doubt
you or your abilities. How can you doubt what
you know to be true? Why you allow others to
influence your sense of self? Turn off the babel,
the noise from other's opinions. Listen only to
your one true voice. Listen to your inner
wisdom, your truth, for it is the only thing you
need to hear.

Follow your flow. Follow your heart. Your inner self will guide you best. Hold yourself true to you and to no other. Your path is clear ahead of you. It is for you to follow. Go. Wander. Seek. Enjoy. Discover. Let your soul guide your footsteps, guide the pace and the rhythm of your stride. Go with confidence, it is your path after all. No one else, only you know the true course you are to follow.

You have the answers to the questions you have asked. Which do you feel have not been answered to your satisfaction? Ah, that is it isn't? Your satisfaction. Not that you haven't been given your answers, but perhaps they are not the answers you're looking for, understand, or want to believe.

Go where you are guided. Take away what means most to you. Leave what does not for others or for another time. What is meaningless or of no value today may be worth a fortune tomorrow. It is time to find the answers that you seek for today.

Why are you blocking the thoughts that are coming to you? All are valuable thoughts, all have meaning to you, for you, in some way. Not all thoughts are preferred, but each has a reason, a meaning, no matter how small. They exist. Honor them. Hear them and then let them go. Their significance will be apparent to you when the time comes and they are needed. Many things, many thoughts run through your mind. Some occur over and over again because you have not examined them. You haven't learned or acknowledged the true message they are meant to bring. So slow down. Allow the thoughts, the messages to come. Fully. Completely. Watch the movies in your head and truly watch. Once you have gotten what is needed, the thought, the dream will no longer exist for it has served its purpose.

What are you looking for? Words of wisdom? You need not seek any further than yourself. Look inside. You have all the answers you need. Seek no further than your own heart. Your own truth. You have a higher wisdom than you allow yourself to believe. You have wisdom that others seek daily. Why not use that truth, that wisdom for yourself? Break free of this self-imposed prison. Find the world you seek. Re-kindle your own spark. Trust in what you do. Trust that you do it well. Trust in who and what you are. Begin now. Listen now. Your heart has your answers.

Look inward. Find the answers you seek. They are there, you just have to look. Hear your inner voice, the one that speaks to you and you alone. You must follow your inner wisdom. You must not allow yourself to go astray. It is a tiny voice with very big message. Listen closely.

Today is the day you begin. Concentrate. Listen. Hear. Hear with your heart. Hear with your soul. See. Feel. Hear. It is in your grasp. It is who you are. You have known this down in your soul. You have always known this. But you have held back because of others, of what they might think, of what they might say. Release yourself from that bondage, that cage that is no longer needed. You are in control of your life, of your body. You need answer to no one for you <u>are</u> the answer. Allow yourself the gift, all of the gifts you were given to use, to enjoy, to honor by using them.

You seek words of wisdom. But what of the wisdom that lives within? You have it there inside you. All answers are there if you just look. Quiet yourself. Slow the chatter of the day. Silence the conversations going on in your mind. Breathe in. Breathe out. Exhale all negative thoughts, all disquieting energies. Breathe in the calm and quiet. That will help you to focus. You are one with the universal spirit. You are your own higher power. Brilliance is within you. Light is within you. Allow the truth you seek to fall within your reach. Allow the answers to float forward into your consciousness, into your waking mind. All other information will float to the side and make way for you have asked and you shall be answered.

Will you make a difference in your world?

Most definitely. What difference you ask? Will you save the world? No. Will you help it evolve? Yes. Every being that moves for the greatest good makes a change, increases the energy, adds to the flow. Choose to use what you have been given. Choose to let it remain as it has been and do nothing. Neither choice is good nor evil. But a choice must be made. Listen to your senses, listen to yourself. Listen fully, deeply, as completely as you never have before. Sense the self of inner you. Do you accept what you feel? Do you sense where you should go? Which path is right? Which is right for you? The answer, your answer will be revealed.

Follow your heart. You should always do that. It is something that you have known for a long time. Let your heart guide you. You know what is right and true without anyone telling you any different. Do not let others influence you as they have their own agendas and interpretations of matters that may not be aligned with your path, your heart. It is okay to feel what you have been feeling. It may not always be painless, but it is never wrong.

Open your heart. Open your soul. Accept the positive energies that are flowing towards you. This moment, this time is one that you have been waiting for, asking for. You can see all points falling into place. All is being aligned. Feel the difference? Sense the balance? No dis-ease, no dis-comfort, no dis-chord. This is your time for ease of understanding. Time to be comfortable in the knowledge that you are where you should be - in harmony with the flow.

This is your time. Time for changing. Time for growth. Time for experience. Do not think too much. Do not react too much. Respond with your heart. Go with your gut as you say. Allow your intuition, your instincts guide you. Listen to yourself. Listen to your guides. Listen to your heart. The answer will be there. You will see the future unfolding. Opening like a flower. You will watch it all and see it accordingly. Know that it is happening and that it is going as it should be – as you have seen it, dreamt it, envisioned it – all those many times.

...BLESSINGS

Patience is not necessary. Acceptance is what is needed. Accept they are coming. Accept that they will come when the time is at hand, and they will be here. All Blessings will be delivered. Accept and allow.

Prepare. Relax and prepare. You know good things are coming. Prepare for them to arrive. Do not fret over the how, the when or even the why. Those do not matter. It is not yours to choose the method. It is yours to prepare and accept. These are gifts. As in all gifts, do you demand what wrapping paper is chosen? What color is used? Do you pick out the card that accompanies it? Would you refuse it if was in blue wrapping and hand carried and not in purple spotted paper delivered by UPS? It is a gift. You would accept it, receive it and appreciate it for what it was no matter what covering it may have had. Your life is such a gift. Blessings will come in many packages, bags and boxes. Many different wrappings will cover each and every one. Blessings will be small. Blessings will be large. Some blessings may bring a tear to your eye. Some will take your breath away. The most precious will make you smile down to your soul. One of those is already on its way to you. And it will arrive when you least expect it. So, stop "expecting" it on your terms. Let the delivery come as it will, when it will. Let those energies flow freely for they do their best work when you do. Prepare to be blessed and in that preparation, let go of the need to control. Prepare to let go and let it happen. For it will – but only if you allow it to.

You know that you are supplied
with everything you need for your life, for your path. Consider it supplied and it will appear. Friendship, love, companionship all three will be yours, <u>are</u> yours. There for you as will be always. That connection will never fade, will never go empty, unfulfilled. Ask and it shall be given. Just ask.

Each time you question, and time you doubt, you slow your progress. You make a step back on your path. It is normal to wonder, but do not doubt. Do not fear, for that only takes away from your power, your worth, your light. Ask yourself what is missing. Is there in fact anything missing at all? Perhaps you have been looking for lack for so long that you have convinced yourself that lack exists when it truly does not. Perhaps what you lack is the state of "lack" itself. You are immensely blessed. You are provided with all that is in your greatest good. See all that you do have. See all that is coming your way. Nothing is missing. Nothing is less than it should be. All is in its place, just as you knew it would be.

Concentrate on what you have, will have, are meant to have. Release the hold you have on lack. It has been for too long- don't you think? Do not focus on the negative, as there truly is no negative. Your life is a blessed and happy one. Blessings cannot come all at once. How would you appreciate them, analyze them, experience them for what they are if they fell down to you all at the same time? Blessings come to you as they should. Small, simple, single-ly, one at a time so that you can realize exactly what they are and what they contain for you. Then as you look around and you acknowledge each and every one, you can see the wealth that is actually yours. All that is yours, all that you deserve is on its way. Do not question the method. Do not question the timing for it comes to you as it does for a reason. But it will come to you. Look around. Find the blessings that are here for you right now, this moment. All are blessings. You know this, you have just forgotten your focus. Let the rest fall as it may, for blessings will fall upon you. They do each and every day. The universe works exactly as it should. Find your peace in that.

Believe, believe, BELIEVE. Many good things in your life are near. Job, finance, love and home are all in line for wonderful changes. All meant for you. We are celebrating already. Wish you could join us. But we know you soon will be. Be positive, be happy; rejoice as we are rejoicing for you. Can't you hear the party horns?

The time will come when the time comes.
No sooner; no later. Be comfortable with that knowledge. Don't try to rush. Don't try to force. What will be will be in its own time; in its own way. Relax, know that the gift is yours already. So there's no need for a panic state, no need to be anxious. The delivery is already set in motion – it's a done deal. Be at peace with yourself and your life as everything is. See. Acknowledge your blessings as they are many and they are wonderful.

Many blessings will reveal themselves in the days to come. Acknowledge them. Accept them. Allow them and they will be delivered, brought to fruition. The key is to allow. Allowing by removing blockages that you have made.

Where is the confirmation you ask?

Faith is a hard thing. Believing without proof, accepting although there is no evidence, no concrete surface with which to touch. Yes, faith is hard. But it is also strong and powerful. Have faith. Believe that you will be and are happy. Believe love is yours already, that the romance is on its way to you, that the perfect job, that financial gain, that sunny day is yours and is being delivered to you. On its way right now. Believe it to be true. Live like it is true and you will find it sooner than you think. Sooner than you realize that it has happened. But concentrate on the "it's not here yet" or "I don't have it" or "where is it?" and that will be all that you will see, all that you receive. Have faith – you are blessed and are being blessed each and every day. Big ones, little ones, surprising ones - blessings are yours. If you take the time to look for them, you will see just how many truly wonderful blessings there are. Tomorrow – count your blessings – literally – count all the good things you experience, feel, see in your day and celebrate each and every one. Get yourself in the right mindset to receive. Because something big is coming and you don't want to miss a single moment!

Do not be concerned about the details, for they are just that – details. What is yours will come to you in the time it is meant to. All things in their time. It may not be what you want to hear, but it is how it is set. Like your many other blessings, their arrival will come when it is best suited to arrive.

You ask what you should do. What action you should take. Nothing. You should do nothing. All is in place and is coming your way. Doing isn't the answer. Being is. Be yourself. Be in expectation. Be in a state of belief. That is what you must do. If you must act, act as if it is yours already… because it is. The life you want. The life you deserve. The life you wish to live is here with you now, open the door and let it come in. Let go of all doubt. See, hear, plan, dream, think as if it is here for you now. Keep that vision in your mind and it will appear before your eyes.

Believe. Allow and it will appear. So much is ready to come your way. All at the horizon to appear at any minute. You can feel it can't you. The words to describe it aren't right, but you feel their near-ness. Unleashing. Freeing. Unbinding. Release is on the edge, nearly here. Closer than right around the corner. Within reach. You can't describe it, but you know and recognize the feeling, the emotion. It is real. <u>All blessings are coming.</u> Believe. Know. Accept. Allow.

As you move with the flow, you will make it easier. Do not fight with the natural order. Do not try to force it. Only this will help things along. Go about your day knowing it will happen, but not searching for the moment. Let it come naturally. For come it will. Your ease of person. Your flow of life. Your ability to live in the moment will be what attracts it, what allows it to happen. Static, needy energy only serves to block, to create a barricade. Relax. Enjoy. Allow.

Lines are connecting; worlds are aligning.
All is making ready. Preparations are almost complete. Do not worry. Do not fret. Do not try to figure things out. Just allow them to happen. Positive thought. Positive mindset. Smile. Be happy. Be the beautiful soul that you are. That is all that is necessary. That is all that is needed. Do not stand in watch. Do not wait. Do not expect or anticipate. No details. No anything, just live your life. No more thoughts about anything other than how wonderful your life is and how wonderful you feel living it. Let your inner light shine as it does, as it should. Live in the moment, for each moment. Full and complete. Turn off your brain. Turn off the logic. Let your heart be free. Let it soar. Let it run wild. The universe is calling you to play. To celebrate. To live pure and free. – What's your answer?

All is taken care of. All that is needed will be provided. This you know already. This you must continue to believe. Believe in this for all things. It works on all levels, for all needs and desires. Remove your doubts. Remove the blocks you have built. Feel the flow, allow its connection to move through your life. Sail the river. Enjoy the ride. It's time to believe again. Truly believe. It is time to allow again. It is time, know that it is time. Do not create unnecessary delays in reaching your destination, your goal.

You are blessed and will be blessed each and every day. Some blessings will be big, some will be small, but watch for them as they are important. They will show you what is to happen next. You will see things in a new light. You will go to new places, do new things. Life will be exciting. Don't worry about the details. They change with every decision that is made, so stop thinking about things and just allow it to happen.

Now is the beginning. The time for beginnings is now. Know that above all, this is your time. Yes, blessings that you have asked for will be revealing themselves in the days to come. Acknowledge them, accept them, allow them and they will be delivered; brought to fruition. The key is to allow. By allowing, you remove the blocks that you have created around you.

...CREATE

Keep doing as you are. Making strides. Keep moving forward. No more looking back. No more "Oh, if only's". No more tears. They are no longer necessary. Close your eyes and visualize. Bring the image of what you wish to be forward in your mind. You will know, you will realize that it is to come. That it is more than a dream. Create your reality. Visualize. Believe. Create.

Happiness is yours to claim. Just claim it. Enjoy it. Own it. Hold it in your heart and it will multiply ten-fold just as the Law of Attraction proclaims. Manifest your destiny. Imagine. Believe. Create. And Enjoy.

Each story has a life of its own, sometimes it flows and grows all by itself, sometimes it takes a little nurturing to bring it along. Just like any project you may take on, there are endless possibilities of how to accomplish what you seek. Just be willing to explore those possibilities.

What do you dream when you close your eyes? Do you dream in wonder? Do you dream at all? What do you dream when your eyes are open? That, my dear, is the most important dreaming to be done. Dreams are not meant to be films you run in your head to replay thoughts and emotions held back from the waking world. Dreams are what you use to create your world. You want more in your life than you have now? Start dreaming. You want to experience new and exciting things? Start dreaming. Imagine what could be there for you at all times. Imagine it as clearly as you can. Dream it into being. Allow yourself to create all the positive possibilities for you to enjoy, for you to become. Then enjoy them. Become them. Not only <u>Dream</u>, but <u>Do</u>. Dreaming is just the start of doing, of <u>BE</u>-ing. See yourself there. BE there with every fiber of yourself. Experience it as clearly as you can. Feel it. Hear the sounds around you. Smell the scents that are there. Fully immerse yourself in your dream. Don't hold back. This is YOUR dream after all. Why stop at just the image, just the snapshot of a possibility? Dive into it with all your heart, all your soul. Let yourself fly. Let yourself soar. Live in the moment you have created for yourself. Before you know it, it will no longer be a dream. It will be your reality. Isn't it amazing what you can do?

Dream. Daydream. Pretend if you must, but keep that vision in your head. See yourself living the life you wish for. Feel it. You must use every part of your imagination. Immerse yourself in your dreams. You've opened the door, now you must widen it by believing that it is on its way. See the wonderful things you will be doing. Plan the trips you will be taking. Act as if "someday" is here today. Create. Believe. Enjoy.

You are powerful. You know this, you have always known this. Be powerful now. Claim what is yours to claim. Claim the happiness. Claim the fortune. Claim the love and the life that is meant for you and only you. You are the creator. You are the artist, the orchestrator of your existence. Create what you want, what you desire, what you deserve. Claim all that is yours. All the best is yours. Be not afraid to claim your inheritance. It is your right. Claim it. Own it. Have it.

The more focused you become with what you do or do not want, the easier it will be for you to bring that into your life. Weed the through the chaff, choose the best and only the best. Make your selection from the best of the grains, not from the weeds you've thrown away.

Learn to change the language of your desires and they will be here for you. They will happen. Be precise, be positive. Show your belief that they already exist and they will.

...CHANGES

Your interests are changing. Your focus has changed because soon your life will be changing. All is good. All is positive. But the focus, the places you find yourself, will be in another place, another format, another mindset than what you have known. Your talents will bring you far and you will touch many lives. Many more than you have already. Are you ready to begin? Very well. Which is good because you know – you already have.

Opportunity is yours. It is coming your way. Do not fear it. Do not doubt it. The door is unlocked and your hand is on the knob. Soon it will turn and the door will swing open and you will find yourself on the other side.

Change is hard sometimes, is it not? But without change what would life be? Things grow. People grow. The world moves on. Your changes are coming. They are just beginning. Your butterfly moments have arrived. Go out in the world embracing the change. Revel in the new. New you, new confidence, new existence. Every day brings a gift. Some bring several. It is time to claim those gifts. Time to open the package and look inside. The universe has much to offer. You have only to open what's inside. Enjoy, for your life is just beginning, as it does with each new day.

Closed doors, open doors, this is what's happening in your life right now. Old doors are closing. New ones are opening up. You wanted to try new things for this year, remember? So, go somewhere new today. Do something new tomorrow. Change things to do a little each day. Bring yourself out of your rut.

Many changes are coming. Good changes, happy changes, but changes none the less. You must be ready for them. They will come fast and furious. Do not get caught off guard. Do not be surprised when they happen. Just go with the flow of positive energies. All are happening, all are done for a reason. Some may feel wrong at first, but you know that the universe has way of balancing and all will work for the greatest good you will be pleased with the results if not the ride. Trust in yourself and follow your instincts. Follow your heart. Follow your gut. You will know which is best and what to do when the time comes. You will be where you should be each and every time. Do not second-guess. Trust, listen, follow through.

You are antsy tonight for a reason. You feel nervous, excited but you are not sure where to go or what to do about it. It's okay and to be expected. Your time, that time is drawing near. You know it. You have felt it coming. Changes are on the horizon this is your time of changes. Your time of moving forward, of new beginnings. It is all good. All that you expected, all that you have dreamed of and more is on its way. All will be there for you experience. Enjoy, delight in it, savor it. Oh my, how you will smile.

Growth is good. Too much familiar, too much similar is not. Do not fear the times of change. Change is necessary to keep you moving forward. Your path contains so much more. Step forward and see what lies ahead.

So much to learn. So much to know.

So much to communicate. You feel it don't
you? – the need, the urgency, the wish to have
knowledge passed on to you. Humans can be
so strange, so funny. You wish to know, but
fear that knowledge at the same time. Growing
is a challenge. The fear of something new, the
fear of the unknown many times cancels the
thirst to learn and grow. Which do you wish in
your heart of hearts? Which do you desire
more – sameness or growth? Knowledge and
wisdom or maintaining life as it is? It's your
decision. It's your choice. You can say yes and
move ahead. You can say no and stay here. It
makes no difference in the outside world. It
will make an outstanding difference in yours.

Life will be changing for you. It has begun already. Bit by bit, piece by piece, changes are being made. Soon what you know as your life will be no more. This is good. Change is good. Change is growth. You will be doing new things, meeting new people, planning new plans. You will pursue new interests, find new likes. How, you ask. You already know the answer. You are not done. Even though you are trying to convince yourself that you are. You are not. You feel it, don't you? The feeling of 'this isn't right anymore". Yes, it's time for a change. Changes are coming. You are at that shift, that moment of pause at the top of the hill on a roller coaster just before you go over and feel the true excitement of the ride. Opportunities abound. Just watch for them and accept them as they arrive. Your life is moving forward while others will stay in place. It is their time for reflection. It is your time to advance, to grow, to become. Watch. Keep your eyes open. Many chances, many advancements, many movements forward. These are for you and you alone. Enjoy them. Cherish them. Honor them as they will honor you.

Your faith and energy will keep you strong. It is one of your best attributes. Keep that faith for you will find your way to happiness. Changes are coming we know but these are changes long in coming, long in developing. Changes that are meant to happen. For without this change you would never know what is coming to you next. And what's next will be amazing. Do not grieve what you are leaving, honor what you have learned and use it moving forward. Yes, it has been a lifetime. But it is time for your life to change, to grow, to become. To become something amazing. God has a purpose for you in his time and his place. The time has come. The place will find you. Do not worry. Do not fret. You are wrapped in His light. Feel the warmth of His love, feel the safety of His arms. Be sure for it is so.

Changes are in progress. Changes are always in progress. Some just happen at different rates than others. You will soon experience several at once. Good changes, positive changes. Your life will be very different, very soon. You will look back and not recognize the life you are living at this moment. Do not worry, all is for your greatest good. All changes are for positive reasons. Yes, you will succeed. Of course you will. You have that power within you. You, as many others, create the life you want. It is all a matter of knowing what you desire and knowing it will come.

Your time is coming, believe that you are in the midst of change and it will show itself soon. Release and it will be revealed. Relinquish and it will be delivered. Remove all doubt for it is yours. Enjoy your life as it is, each moment as it is. That energy will help attract what you need. Being you at your best, at your highest joy and only joy will follow.

You will start anew today. Things that held your interest will no longer. Things you hadn't thought about will come into focus. New things, new changes. Communications will come to you. Abilities will reveal themselves. Grow. Evolve. Change. Embrace the new and different. Challenge yourself. Challenge others to grow as well. Expand your world. Become limitless.

You feel it, don't you? The change that is coming. The change to your life. A change to everything that you know it today.   Do not fear it. Do not worry. The change is good. The change is for your greatest good. You sense it because the energies around you are changing; preparing for you. Yes, many changes are occurring. All are good. All are yours to claim. Release yourself and allow the changes to occur. It is time for you to move on and realize your fullest potential.

Your story is about to begin. Your path is widening and will soon include a new, a broader experience in your life's journey. You will be taken to where you have never been before. Do not be frightened, for this is all good. This is all growth for you. Hold on to your faith. Follow your heart. Breathe. Listen. Do not try to fill in the words of this message. Allow this message to fill you. Much will happen. You will not recognize yourself or your life for all the changes that are on the path before you. Take each step as it comes. The journey will astound you. Be in each moment. Do not miss the beauty because you decided to rush along the path. The path is yours and is meant for you to travel. For you to experience. The blessings are in the lessons that you will learn along the way.

Always know that you are loved.

Made in the USA
Columbia, SC
14 January 2018